Praise for **Because**

"It's our joy to partner with biblically-functioning, relationally-healthy visionaries and missionaries like the Rileys, who love the local church and lead us towards the lost."

*Alan Scott, Senior Leader at Causeway Coast Vineyard
Coleraine, Northern Ireland*

"Mark and Beccy are brilliant! They are passionate lovers of Jesus and they are full of desire to see many young people brought into a relationship with Jesus. Their determined hard work and careful stewarding of what God has given them has seen some fantastic doors open up on the North Coast. Their willingness to walk out what they believe is both inspiring and challenging to all who look on. I am delighted to be able to endorse Mark and Beccy, and am excited to see what God does with them next!"

*Ian Hannah, Director of Music at Portstewart Baptist Church
Portstewart, Northern Ireland*

becauseyou'reloved

MARK NATHAN RILEY

A PAIS MOVEMENT RESOURCE

BECAUSE YOU'RE LOVED
Copyright © 2016 by Mark Nathan Riley

Published by Harris House Publishing
www.harrishousepublishing.com
Colleyville, Texas
USA

Available on amazon.com and paismovement.com/resources.

This title is also available in other formats.
Cover creation and design by Matt Adams from www.fallendesign.com
Author's photo by Joshua McMichael Photography

All scripture quotations, unless otherwise indicated, are taken from the Holy Bible,
New International Version®, NIV®. Copyright ©1973, 1978, 1984, 2011 by Biblica,
Inc.™ Used by permission of Zondervan. All rights reserved worldwide.
www.zondervan.com The "NIV" and "New International Version" are trademarks
registered in the United States Patent and Trademark Office by Biblica, Inc.™

Cataloging-in-Publication Data

Riley, Mark Nathan, 1982 -
        Because You're Loved / Mark Nathan Riley
            p.cm.
        Includes bibliographical references
        ISBN 978-0-9862831-8-5 (pbk.)
        1. Christianity and Culture. 2. Christian Life. I. Title.

Printed in the United States of America.

For Beccy and my family,
Who make the adventure beautiful, fun, and exciting.

With special thanks to:

Beccy, the beauty and brains of our family.

Our boys, Zach, Levi, and Micah, and their tireless energy.

Paul and Lynn for their friendship, guidance, and direction over the years.

Matt Adams of www.fallendesign.com for all of his design magic since the beginning of BYL.

My parents, Paul and Jenny, for all they have invested in me, cheering me on and policing my grammar.

The Days and Kitcheners for all their support and care.

Harris House Publishing for the opportunity to resource more missionaries.

Contents

Foreword
By Paul Clayton Gibbs

Why are you a Christian?

It is probably for the same reason anyone else is... Someone, at some point, told you about Jesus. Someone knew you were loved.

Now there may, of course, be various reasons why you decided to *accept* Christ. However, without someone speaking about Jesus, showing you Jesus, and bringing you to Jesus, it is unlikely that you would have known about the possibility.

> *"How, then, can they call on the one they have not believed in? And how can they believe in the one of whom they have not heard? And how can they hear without someone preaching to them?" (Romans 10:14)*

At Pais, our desire is to be missionaries who make missionaries, and that passion has no better example than the life and work of Mark Riley. With his wife Beccy, he has taken the teaching of Pais and created an idea that first touched thousands in his homeland of Northern Ireland. Then with open hands, he worked with us to remodel it, creating a method that has now motivated tens of thousands of people around the world to speak, share, and bring people to faith.

It is a simple campaign with three missions and can be used with believers and non-believers alike. I encourage you, therefore, to read about the heart behind Because You're Loved and use it in your workplace, college, school, or neighbourhood in order to give people the greatest opportunity they will ever know... the choice to accept Christ for themselves.

Thank you, Mark, for your idea and for your generosity!

Paul Clayton Gibbs is the Founder and Global Director of Pais, an international movement of missionaries making missionaries. A visionary who seeks to advance the Kingdom of God, Paul pioneered Pais as an inter-denominational youth and schools ministry, and has overseen its expansion into churches and businesses covering six continents. Paul teaches throughout the world on topics which include pioneering, leadership development, and the Kingdom of God.

www.paismovement.com

#becauseyoureloved

Part 1

Why It's Important

HEART

Questions

Most journeys begin with choices, and in my experience many choices begin with questions.

In 2010, my family and I embarked on a journey with Pais Ireland that could be best described as an adventure. Along the roller coaster of this adventure, questions gave birth to innovation, and Because You're Loved (BYL) was birthed as an initiative to mobilise people for everyday mission in their worlds.

For months, we had sensed God stirring us for a new chapter in life. Then my wife Beccy and I, along with our two young boys (we've had a third since), moved from my hometown of Manchester, England, to the North Coast of Northern Ireland, becoming missionaries with the Pais Movement for the second time. Our first apprenticeship and time on staff with Pais was incredibly influential in our approach to life, in particular igniting a passion in our hearts for engaging our community, wherever that might be, with the love of Christ. Although it was hard leaving family and friends and beginning a new adventure with two toddlers in tow and no certainty of a regular wage, one question defined our decision.

In Manchester, I had been in a band called "Our Empire." It was a fitting name. We completely went it alone, having generated our own fan base, recorded our own EP, booked our own gigs, and promoted as best we could. Without producers and management, we really were our own empire, and it was fun, especially when things began to gain momentum. As my wife and I began exploring what a new chapter of life may look like, I wrestled with an all too profound question:

His Kingdom or Our Empire?

Each day we all make hundreds of choices that answer that very same question. Even today, I am continually challenged by what my choices say about my answer. I am compelled by the question:

What might our communities look like if we model, heart and soul, the answer, "His Kingdom?"

Not only that, but also:

What might our communities look like if we empower and equip our worlds to model this answer to their worlds too?

Questions like these are dangerous because they lead to other questions. Questions like, do our current expressions of evangelism really work? For many years, the Pais Movement has identified, explored, and shaped conversations around this question. One of the values that significantly resonated with us as we explored what the next chapter of our lives might look like was Pais' underlying belief that a fresh approach to mission is required, that we must go beyond a model of attraction to application, that it isn't enough to simply create polished, entertaining, attractive events. Our world needs something far more wide-reaching. At the core of Pais, we believe we must empower and engage disciples and followers of Christ to carry Him into their schools, colleges, workplaces, families, and communities.

I have found there are two common perceptions in contemporary Christian circles about sharing our faith. Some consider it to be an entirely personal thing and so believe it has no place in a public context. Alternatively and more positively, sharing our faith is considered by some to have relevance but only for those to whom it fits as a gift, such as an evangelist. You have probably heard these concepts many times, but what if both still miss the point?

What if God's perspective is different? Could it be that we all have the capacity to be world changers in the here and now? For example, youth ministry is often seen as preparing young people in our church families for their future as adults. But what might our communities look like, what might our schools look like, what might our churches look like, if we empower them to be a now generation? What if rather than simply surviving their teenage years and retaining enough faith to stay in church through university and into adulthood, they have a part to play in engaging their friends, families, and peers with Jesus? Similarly, I have come across the perception that skilled men or women in business roles in our churches are to release finances into the Kingdom. But what might our communities look like, what might our business sector look like, what might our churches look like, if we empower them within their spheres of influence? What if rather than simply releasing money into the Kingdom and retaining enough of a pick-me-up from Sunday services to make it through the week, they have a part to play in engaging their friends, colleagues, clients, and peers with Jesus?

The reality is everyone can evangelise. Everyone does it all the time about everyday stuff. Yet no one goes on a six week course to learn how to share their favourite music, fashion, or TV show! The key is getting the concepts of sharing the gospel into a context that makes it relatable, accessible, and doable.

In 2010, as the windy, damp, grey Irish winter began to set in, a few of us from Pais Ireland sat huddled around a half-working electric heater in the back room of a coastal church hall. The question of how to do this was bursting in our chests and evolved into a much further reaching conversation. How could we create something that could facilitate more people sharing their experiences, their stories or their discoveries as they engage with the Kingdom? As we discussed what we could do and bounced ideas off each other, slowly the concept for BYL began to form.

Gamechanger

Having been privileged to grow up in church, I have seen a number of expressions of 'mission' over the years.

For a while it was very common to hear street preachers broadcasting the immediate dangers of Hell's fire. At some point, however, influential Christians suggested evangelism based on the terrors of Hell may in fact be putting people off church. Subsequently, seeker-friendly initiatives were birthed.

I remember doing local community service projects as a teenager, wondering if anyone really knew why I was painting their fence. We had polarised so far from terror-based evangelism I think many may have simply thought I was on community service. (To be fair my appearance probably did not help.) Frankly, I found it all a bit disillusioning. How could we be content with painting someone's fence while inside they went hungry because of illness preventing them from working? Was the goal to leave feeling reassured that at least in this life they would have a nice fence to look at? Surely they needed more, and surely an encounter with Jesus would change more.

When I look at the gospels and read about Jesus moving from town to town, I notice a fascinating model. Jesus seldom mentioned Hell, yet He does not make His message easy to accept either. He spoke within a cultural context, yet His listeners often had to search for His meanings. He mostly spoke of His Kingdom, yet never directly resisted Roman occupation. Far from polarisation, Jesus carved out a path of paradox.

Paradox makes many of us uncomfortable. How can two opposites exist at the same time? Can we be seeker-friendly and up front at the same time? Can we love with no strings and yet initiate discovery? Can we be proactive without being aggressive?

Jesus is a game changer. He is the kind of friend who if you arranged to meet for a coffee you should pack a toothbrush and a spare pair of underwear (although he'd probably tell you not to bring anything for the road) because you never know what might happen. The disciples went on all sorts of wild adventures with Him in the Bible. Preaching trips, healings, exorcisms, divine provisions of food, finance and business, transfiguration, weather control, defying the laws of physics, and righteous vandalism all happened, but everywhere He went people came alive. Tax collectors, prostitutes, terrorists, beggars, blind, lame, deaf, mute, outcasts, even the dead were all transformed in some way when they encountered Jesus. Jesus is a game changer.

When I was younger I followed my local football team, Manchester United, full of hope and expectation. Sometime before I was born they had been one of the most successful teams in the UK, but their success had dwindled and when I started following them they wallowed somewhere near the bottom of their league. Yet hope emerged in the form of a new manager, and I watched as season after season he made improvement after improvement and brought a once glorious team back to the top of the league. One of the manager's most successful tactics was his super subs, but there was one in particular whom he would bring onto the pitch with ten or so minutes to go. United's most famous super sub was nicknamed "The Baby-faced Assassin" and is most celebrated for clinching a remarkable comeback in the 1999 European Champions League Final, leading Manchester United on to win their third major league title. In footballing terms, he was a game changer; when he came off the bench, very often matches like that Champions League Final would completely turn around just at the crucial moment.

Some years ago, preparing for one of Pais Ireland's early Because You're Loved weeks, I was in a late night prayer meeting. While we prayed, I saw what I can only describe as a vision; I don't experience things like that very often so it etched itself into my memory. I saw a large sports hall in front of me. There were hundreds, maybe thousands, of people kneeling, faces to the floor with their heads buried in their hands. I looked on as someone moved through the room. He had his back to me but something about Him emanated righteousness and goodness; it was as if these qualities shone from Him like light. As He moved through the room, He touched individuals on the shoulders and as they rose they were greeted with a warm embrace. They were facing me and I could make out huge beaming smiles or tears of joy streaming as they celebrated in His embrace. It was in this moment I felt God clearly say, "I long for you to introduce them to Me. I will embrace them and they will know the warmth of My love."

It was a defining moment as I vowed I was no longer content with just training our teams to deliver slick presentations or clever ways of convincing anyone God was real. Instead I realised that introductions are the catalysts for life transformation. It is Jesus who is the game changer and an encounter with Him changes everything.

Near

While He was on Earth, Jesus often made statements like, "The Kingdom is near." For example, He sends His disciples out telling them:

> "As you go, proclaim this message: 'The kingdom of heaven has come near.'" (Matthew 10:7)

I grew up believing this was a reference to the second coming. I am fairly certain this was taught to me at some point, but my memory of Sunday school is a little hazy. Something bothered me about that interpretation for years. Over two thousand years on, give or take a few, the truth of that statement seemed a little questionable. Few explanations satisfied me, not even quotes from Psalms:

> *"A thousand years in your sight are like a day that has just gone by, or like a watch in the night."* (Psalm 90:4)

I am sure I am not alone with questions like this. What if Jesus was not referring to a future timescale but in fact His statement had everything to do with the here and now? Could He in fact be suggesting the Kingdom was within our reach, within our grasp, that the Kingdom was close at hand?

It makes much more sense. He sends the disciples out giving them authority over sickness and the demonic:

> *"Heal the sick, raise the dead, cleanse those who have leprosy, drive out demons. Freely you have received; freely give."* (Matthew 10:8)

He makes huge promises like:

> *"Very truly I tell you, whoever believes in me will do the works I have been doing, and they will do even greater things than these, because I am*

> *going to the Father. And I will do whatever you ask in my name, so that the Father may be glorified in the Son. You may ask me for anything in my name, and I will do it." (John 14:12-14)*

I believe these statements are as true today as they were when first spoken.

The Merriam-Webster Dictionary defines Kingdom as, in part:

> *a: a realm or region in which something is dominant*
>
> *b: an area or sphere in which one holds a preeminent position*

Put more simply, Kingdom means where the rule, the reign, and the sovereignty of an individual is recognised. So the Kingdom of Heaven is wherever God is recognised.

Jesus taught us to pray:

> *"Your kingdom come, your will be done, on earth as it is in heaven." (Matthew 6:10)*

Jesus also said:

> *"Very truly I tell you, the Son can do nothing by himself; he can do only what he sees his Father doing, because whatever the Father does the Son also does." (John 5:19)*

These statements have everything to do with God's will being done. It is not a stretch of the imagination to suggest that Jesus gives us a glimpse of God the Father's will. What did Jesus do? Heal the sick, set the captives free, heal the brokenhearted, and selflessly spend Himself for us.

Albeit a simplistic summary, at the core of salvation, Jesus (in very essence God and yet in the form of man) selflessly sacrificed His life to buy our freedom to connect with Father God. Salvation comes through our surrendering of our own will and placing God the Father as sovereign in our lives. And as sovereign in our lives, He comes and lives in our hearts.

Therefore it seems like it should be inconceivable that we show up at someone's house to paint a fence and simply paint a fence. If we have placed Him sovereign in our lives, then we must expect His will to far exceed our rational expectations. I think we have missed the point somewhat if we think that it would be God's will for someone to have a neatly painted fence but still be held captive by worry, limp on crutches, or go hungry. Maybe that sounds extreme, but essentially that is the byproduct of passive evangelism.

Similarly, it would seem we've missed the point if we think that it would be God's will for someone to be so terrified of Hell that we help them to neatly spruce up their life through a list of rules and yet still be held captive by worry and merely learn to cope with sickness or hunger. Again extreme, but often, this is what aggressive evangelism has achieved as a byproduct.

What might our communities look like if we dared to take Jesus at His word?

What might our communities look like if we have a part to play in heaven coming to earth in the here and now?

What if we can facilitate encounters?

At the heart of BYL and the Pais Movement is an adventurous fist-in-the-air cry to go beyond attraction to application, resonating with the nearness of the Kingdom, refusing to be held back by risk or polarisation. A calling to people young and old to make His Kingdom their primary concern, to mobilise and take ownership for their worlds in the present day.

It is clearly and specifically designed to be an alternative approach to mission. Make no mistake, it does not exist solely to connect anyone to a building, organisation, or gathering; instead, it exists to equip and empower a multitude of everyday missionaries to discover the heart of the King and facilitate discovery of His Kingdom.

At first we very much learnt by trial and error. We experimented and analysed and processed our experiences to find the most effective ways of achieving our goals. We made everything we were working on available to anyone who wanted it and it wasn't long before, with the help of Paul Gibbs, the Pais Movement

Global Director, teams started reproducing BYL projects around the world. Since then we have worked closely with Paul Gibbs and Michael Davies, Training Director of the Pais Movement. Together we've been able to shape, develop, and disseminate our ideas to and through the wider Pais Movement. BYL continues to grow from month to month, having become a mission outreach that has moved from just Pais Ireland to cities, towns, and villages throughout the world. As a programme that fuels community outreach, BYL now touches many more people than Pais Ireland ever could have on our own.

In practice, Because You're Loved is simply indiscriminate acts of love as an outlet for the unconditional love He has shown us. 1 John 4:19 puts it very simply:

"We love because he first loved us."

And it really is simple! Perform an act of kindness—wash a neighbour's car, pay for someone's shopping, leave a chocolate bar on someone's desk, pray for someone sick, share a word straight from God's heart, etc.—and pass on a BYL card afterwards.

The card simply has the BYL web address on it and is designed to promote conversation. Importantly, these should be intentional conversations, opportunities for individuals to share their stories and their experiences of God's love with the aim of facilitating encounters with Father God who lives in us! I hope for these encounters to be tangible experiences of God's great love for many who do not yet know Him.

BYL is a holistic approach to evangelism that can be done any way, any time, anywhere, and with anyone. It has been reproduced on six continents. To help mobilise a movement, we have devised three separate week-long programmes to show, share, and bring people to faith. These programmes are meant to take place over the course of a year and can be done in any order. Resources and videos are available through our corresponding website, www.becauseyoureloved.com/how.

Throughout all of our programmes runs a deeply rooted value for empowering volunteers not only to engage in acts of service, generosity, or leading conversations, but to use those as launch pads for creating encounters with Jesus. The apostle Paul wrote in 1 Corinthians 2:3–5:

> "*I came to you in weakness with great fear and trembling. My message and my preaching were not with wise and persuasive words, but with a demonstration of the Spirit's power, so that your faith might not rest on human wisdom, but on God's power.*"

Those short few verses very much resonate with our heart for Because You're Loved as an initiative. Who knows? One simple act of love could carry the hope someone is desperate for!

Part 2

How It Works

Dared To Love

Show the Faith

Dared to Love (DTL) combines social action with a clear expression of the gospel. Five days with five dares facilitate a week long mobilisation of people in local mission, empowering them as the now generation, each with ownership and responsibility for his or her friends.

When we first started DTL, we gathered close to seventy-five ordinary people to engage with their worlds in this way. Stories filtered back of young people breaking into school lockers and leaving chocolates (we trust no actual damage was done). Another group of university students got together and left daffodils and a card on every car in a local car park. Someone else asked a shopkeeper what their favourite chocolate was and bought it for them. I think what makes it most accessible is the simplicity and the fun of the project.

We made the idea and template for the weeks available across the Pais Movement, and it wasn't long before stories using #becauseyoureloved began surfacing on Facebook and Twitter from projects that I had no idea were taking place. I am pleased to say the impact these projects made paved the way for BYL as a whole becoming the catalytic programme for how Pais teams around the world facilitate ordinary people doing mission in their everyday contexts.

Increasingly we have found ways to use the dares to create opportunities for 'encounters.' Let's be honest, most of us who have been in ministry for any length of time have gotten really good at running service projects, but we are fascinated by what could happen if we go beyond simply serving our communities well to bringing life to our communities.

How might the stories of our communities begin to change if we help people engage with Jesus in environments where they can develop a relationship with the Giver of life?

What could happen if we *show* them what faith in Jesus really looks like?

Earlier this year, a few of my team were running a lesson in a local high school during a DTL week. They shared some of their own personal experiences of God's love, explored a little of what love looks like, and as they broke into small groups for some activities, one young man who had been a little disruptive throughout the class announced that he didn't believe any of their stories and didn't think God existed. Unfazed, my team affirmed that he had the right to believe what he liked. However, they also asked what it would take for him to begin to believe God might exist. His answer was, "If I experience Him."

If you have ever met any of my team, you'd know you can't say things like that around them without something happening. So they asked if he was in any way sick or had any pain in his body. He replied he had torn his hamstring a few days earlier and was in pain from that. So they asked if they could pray for it and he agreed. About a minute in he started freaking out because the back of his leg felt warm and tingly but there was no one touching him, and all of a sudden he blurted out that there was no pain anymore. His friends said, "No way, you're making that up," but he remained adamant he had been healed. At the end of class he was one of six young people who approached the team, asking what they had to do to become Christians, and one of our team led him in a prayer inviting Jesus to be part of his life then and there at the back of class, tears and snot everywhere.

Countless similar stories have filtered back from people who use the cards as a tool to create opportunities to speak hope into their friends' lives or to pray for them. Because of a DTL week, a young lady invited another young lady who had been bullying her in school to come to one of our events where she heard how much

Jesus loved her. There, she invited Jesus to be part of her life and it has not only brought restoration to that situation but she has plugged herself into the life of our youth church community where she is catching God's heart for her world.

Intentionally, we have kept the format as skeletal as possible. The emphasis is a community of believers who engage in a DTL project to add flesh to the bones, so to speak, with their own ideas.

Dared to Love Week

Dared to Love is a week-long project that dares groups of volunteers to show the love of Jesus through indiscriminate acts of service and kindness towards others.

In a nutshell, Dared to Love is about showing God's love in a practical way. We run it as an intentional project based on 1 John 4:19 where we read that, "We love because he first loved us." Over the course of five days, volunteers are sent out to their neighbourhoods, communities, families, and friends to undertake "dares" which fall into five themes, one for each of the five days of the project: encouragement, service, compassion, generosity, and connection. Running a Dared to Love week is quite simple, but requires you to organise, gather, and prepare volunteers before sending them out to do all the hard work!

Launch Night

We usually start a DTL project week with a Launch Night. We find a launch is important to galvanise potential volunteers to sign up and to inspire them to get creative with the dares for the week. The key to a successful launch is a great deal of promotion beforehand to encourage potential participants to come.

The night aims to:

- Inspire and equip volunteers for the week

- Furnish all the information and resources necessary

- Let all the DTL volunteers meet each other

- Develop ideas of how best to make an impact during the week

- Provide an opportunity to worship and learn more about our awesome God!

The best time for a Launch Night would be sometime a week or so before the actual Dared to Love week and should probably last around an hour and a half.

Below is a template of a successful Launch Night we have run previously:

- **Ice Breaker** (10 mins). Give the volunteers a few minutes to get to know each other using big games, questions, etc. Embracing the theme of dares, we ran some dares based on the game show Fear Factor.

- **Worship** (20 mins). Start the night with worship, aiming to get the volunteers focused on and connected with God. A live band playing contemporary, high-energy worship music would be ideal.

- **Provide packs** (2 mins). Provide each of the volunteers with a Dared to Love pack (welcome letter, handout, and at least five Because You're Loved cards) to use over the week. You can find free electronic copies of the welcome letter, handout, and cards via becauseyoureloved.com/how. We strongly advise using a professional print company to ensure quality.

- **Explanation of DTL week** (10 mins). Using a Launch Night PowerPoint, talk through the handout, explaining each of the days, how it works, and what they could do. Encourage them to think outside the box with their own ideas to make the dares their own.

- **Short inspirational talk** (10 mins). Bring in someone to inspire the volunteers with a short, relevant message that preferably provides a Biblical basis for the week.

- **Group discussion** (20 mins). The main part of this Launch Night is to get the volunteers together to develop ideas. Ideally, if you have a number of volunteers from the same area (school, church, business, etc.), split them into these groups and let them discuss how to run the week, collectively or individually, in their own 'mission field.' There is space on the handouts for them to note down their ideas.

- **Chill out time** (10 mins). Try and leave some time at the end for the volunteers to just talk and enthuse each other about the coming week, possibly provide some food, etc. to encourage them to stay and talk.

Printing

You can download free copies of printable resources at www.becauseyoureloved.com/how. Where possible, it is worth estimating the number of people you expect to attend your Launch Night, as each volunteer who signs up should receive a volunteer pack.

There are four things that need to be printed for each volunteer. I strongly recommend having at least the first three parts printed professionally to ensure high quality. It may also be advisable to print more packs than you expect to need. The four things that need to be printed are:

- **Handout**. The DTL handout is a single-sided, A5 or half size, portrait sheet which gives participants a breakdown of the week's dares and a space to note ideas for use during the week.

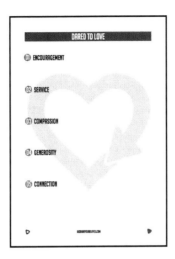

- **BYL cards**. BYL cards (business card size and at least five for each volunteer) need to be printed and inserted into the centre of the pack. The cards are designed to be given out along with an act of kindness.

- **Encouragement postcards**. Business card size BYL postcards have been created for the encouragement dare. At least five for every volunteer need to be printed and inserted into the pack.

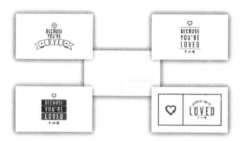

- **Welcome letters**. Welcome letters need to be printed and put together with the handouts to complete the pack.

We also advise including some Dared to Love/Because You're Loved merchandise, t-shirts, badges, stickers, etc., in the packs. Free templates are available for download via becauseyoureloved.com/how.

The Week

The week is when everything happens! Most of it will rely on your volunteers, but we strongly recommend you get involved. Here are some ideas we have used:

- **Flash mob**. These are designed to be fun, raise awareness, and build momentum. Pick a busy time of day in a local retail centre, plant a busker, and make sure all volunteers are aware of the chosen time and song. When the busker starts the specific song (a well-known song reflecting the theme of love), volunteers quickly gather, joining together for the song and dispersing as soon as it is finished. If you feel a bit more ambitious, flash mobs using dance routines are very effective.

- **Activities for volunteers to join in with during the course of the week**. Each day of the week has a respective dare. Why not organise some collective activities that volunteers can take part in?

- **Lunch time gatherings**. Creating something different for people to engage with during their lunch break can be a very positive experience. These can be done in educational, corporate, and community settings. We have used prayer spaces, creative environments where people can explore prayer and faith, drop-in cafes, mini concerts, and food giveaways. The key is to create environments that are fun, creative, and have the opportunity to help people encounter Jesus.

- **Concert**. There are many great Christian performers out there, musicians, theatre productions, comedians, and entertainers. We have found organising a concert as part of a Dared to Love week to be very effective.

- **Street giveaways**. Are there areas of your town or city that see a high volume of people passing through? Street giveaways can be a great way to create a widespread buzz and get your message out far and wide.

- **Family fun days**. Lots of communities have shared spaces that are great for bringing friends, family, and the wider community together for fun filled gatherings and experiences. Bouncy castles, face painting, exotic animals, barbecue, sports activities, prize giveaways, and much more make for great family fun events.

- **Sports competitions**. Sports competitions have a widespread appeal for many, both for participation and watching. They can be a great way to gather a crowd and connect with wider communities.

- **Open mic evenings**. Coffee shops and other shared spaces can be great for gathering small crowds of people who want to perform. They can also be a great way to use the talents of those connected to your project to share the deeper message of God's love.

The Party

We have used an end-of-the-week party, a little like a wrap party. It's a time when we gathered participants and their friends together to celebrate the great things that happened during the week and to spotlight some of the most interesting. One of my favourite that we have done previously was a UV rave. We kitted out a large hall with UV lights and concert lighting and brought in a loud sound system. We set up a Dubstep DJ, gave out glow sticks and UV face paint, and threw a party. Whilst this is a celebration of all that has happened through the course of the week, it is also a great opportunity to reinforce that this is a catalytic week and participants should not stop sharing God's love as they leave, but should continue to aim to engage their friends with Jesus in the days and weeks to come.

The best time for the event is sometime the weekend directly following the project week and could last approximately an hour and a half. The event should incorporate:

- Fun and generosity with a party atmosphere

- Lots of energy, fast-paced

- A place volunteers feel comfortable inviting their friends

- A good communicator of the gospel

- Provision of follow up opportunities like a new believers group. We recommend something like the Alpha Course by Nicky Gumbel, which can be found at www.alpha.org.

- Creative decoration/layout of venue

- Professional quality graphics

You can find free electronic copies of the handout, cards, and all of our designs via becauseyoureloved.com/how. We strongly advise using a professional print company to ensure quality.

Who Loves You?

Share the Faith

Who Loves You? (WLY?) combines a media teaser campaign with the facilitation of opportunities for people to share their stories of faith. It actively encourages people to be creative in local mission and empowers participants to practice a culture of offering encounters with God's love.

It is important for participants to understand their stories are important no matter how dramatic or mundane they seem. They are stories of how the Kingdom is and has advanced in our lifetime; they join with millions of others throughout history and will join with those who are yet to begin a God story. Dramatic content does not make a story any more powerful; the power is in God's transformation and God is transforming lives whether we have been a drug dealer who found faith after Jesus appeared to us whilst we smoked the pages of the Bible or we quietly discovered God's love in the midst of obtaining straight A's and doing charitable work. The important question is: What has God done in our lives? It is important not that we promote a gospel of God as some kind of grandiose personal assistant, but that the cross and resurrection was not the end of God's plans. Our stories of transformation tell of the hope we have not just for the future, but for this life here and now. For those who may find it difficult to know what or where to begin, I advise they just start with why. Why did they choose to invite Jesus into their life and what began to change from that point?

Recently my team took a series of lessons into a school during our most recent WLY? week. The school was just beginning a series of religious education classes, a common part of the curriculum in the UK. The series was about what Christians believe the cross represents. So we shared our stories of what the cross meant to us individually, then we opened it up for the young people to explore what the cross could mean to them. We divided the room into four sections: one section explored forgiveness, another explored who God is, another explored if God could do one thing what they would ask for, and the fourth explored how they could bring hope to their community. As the lesson contin- ued, each section had the opportunity to move around and explore each of the other groups. Many of the answers blew our minds as the young people engaged with many aspects of what the cross represents. We had the privilege of leading three young lads to invite Jesus to be part of their lives at the end of class.

But one story in particular moved me. A week after we had taken those lessons, I heard a story from one of my friend's small groups. Towards the end of the small group two weeks previously, a couple in his group had asked everyone to pray for their son. They were concerned he was showing signs of depression and spending more and more time researching evolution and atheism; they were worried as he seemed to be walking a darker and darker path. Unknown to us, we showed up in his class and began talking about our experiences of God's love. Later that evening when he arrived home, he opened up to his parents about the class and to all of our surprise, he showed up in church later that week. I say surprise because he had actually been the student who seemed most hostile to our message, all the while actually processing a fresh desire to re-engage with God.

Every week my church opens up our building for drop-in cafés. At our teenage drop-in, we gather a small crowd of twenty to thirty who just come hang out, eat toast, play football, and chat. One of our volunteers who faithfully helps out each week took the opportunity to share some of her story with a handful of our younger guests. As she sensed they were leaning in, she opened up the opportunity for them to invite Jesus to be part of their lives too. Eagerly, they accepted and, amidst all the chaos of footballs and young people letting off steam, she led three of them as they invited Jesus to be part of their lives.

Similarly, I recently met another guest, an older gentleman arriving for one of our daytime drop-in café gatherings. It was his first time and in the middle of our large carpark he found himself a little disorientated and wanted me to point him in the right direction for the drop-in. We chatted for a few minutes and I noticed he was using two walking sticks to prop himself up so as politely as possible, I enquired what he needed them for. He explained the terrible pain he suffered from due to various ailments and I wrestled for a moment with the decision to sympathise and walk him to the door or ask if he would like to know Jesus and share one of my own stories of healing and offer to pray for his pain to be healed. I am pleased to say I mustered up the courage and asked if he knew Jesus loved him and I count it as a real privilege I had the opportunity to help him encounter Jesus and wonderfully his pain vanished almost in an instant that morning.

Stories become even more powerful when we offer the opportunity for someone to experience the same. They may not be journeying through the same stuff as we did or are, but our experience of God's love is not dependent on our situations but on the infinite, unfailing, and unconditional nature of His love. Irrelevant of whether their journey is similar to ours, they can experience what we experienced. So we teach our volunteers to share their stories and offer opportunities for people to respond in some way.

Who Loves You Week

A simple question to provoke a deep answer, Who Loves You? is a week-long project that facilitates conversation in order to share God's perfect love for imperfect people.

In short, Who Loves You? is about provoking people to think beyond their immediate situations. Based on Matthew 16:13-20, where Jesus asks His disciples who people say He is, our hope is that this question will provoke a process of thought that leads to a revelation of Jesus as a loving Saviour. Like in this passage, Jesus regularly used questions to provoke deeper understanding.

Who Loves You? is a creative programme of guerilla marketing, media, and events that runs through five days of a week. Volunteers are empowered to share their stories in their neighbourhoods, schools, workplaces, families, and friendship groups.

If you choose to run a Who Loves You? week in your area like our Dared to Love programme, you need to gather, equip, empower, and send out as many volunteers as possible. While I have included some examples that you can use, I would encourage you to use them as templates and produce something tailored for your own area. I recommend beginning to promote your

Who Loves You? project at least one month before you intend to run it.

Once again, promotion of this project is vital. The effectiveness of your promotion will directly affect the success of the week!

The Week

The week is when everything happens! This is when you begin to help people unpack the question and facilitate the beginning a journey of discovery.

During the week, we prefer not to answer the question directly. Instead of teaching the people what to think, we at Pais are committed to teaching people how to think. This is not an excuse to be vague. In fact, it is important to be all the more specific, explicit, and intentional as you guide people to investigate and discover God's love for themselves.

The Event

The event is an integral part of the week and a great way to round off your story telling theme. It provides the opportunity for people to respond to God's love. It is designed to create a point for integration into the church and further discipleship.

The best time for the event is sometime the weekend directly following the project week and could last approximately an hour and a half. The event should incorporate:

- Fun with prize giveaways

- Lots of energy, fast-paced

- Professional standard entertainment in a story telling context (e.g., musician who tells his story through music)

- A place volunteers feel comfortable inviting their friends

- Good communicator/communicators of the gospel through their stories

- Provision of follow up opportunities like a new believers group. We recommend something like the Alpha Course by Nicky Gumbel, which can be found at www.alpha.org

- Creative decoration/layout of venue

- Professional quality graphics

NB. Create an opportunity to get names, numbers, and email addresses. This will help you to follow up on any newcomers and do your best to help them continue to connect with your environment.

Below is an example of one successful event we have previously run:

- **Ice Breaking** (10 mins). A high energy atmosphere should permeate the venue from the start. As people arrive, have a DJ playing music and something eye catching (a skateboard/bmx videos playing on a screen, etc.). Lay the room out with lots of graphics, canvases, lights, etc. Create a Narnia Experience (not with trees); guests should feel like they are walking into a completely different atmosphere.

- **Fun** (5 mins). Start the night with a high-energy, fun game: the messier, the faster paced, the more eye-catching is all the better. (Bear in mind the average age present and ensure you pitch your interaction accordingly.)

- **Live Music** (10 mins). Live band, the best quality you can find, to play energetic contemporary music.

- **Video** (2 mins). Previously, we made a short video exploring the question: Who loves you? Details can be found on page 55.

- **Giveaway** (3 mins). In keeping with the Because You're Loved context, be as generous as possible. Be an unexpected blessing.

- **Freestyle football performance** (25 mins). Mix in a footballer talking about what he does, involving the audience, and teaching volunteers new tricks. Within that context, the footballer can incorporate the story of how he found and honed his gift and direction in life through discovering and encountering Jesus.

- **Creative** (5 mins). Try to find a creative way to set the speaker up for sharing their stories. You could incorporate videos, music, stories, art, photography, or anything you like.

- **Short inspirational story teller** (5 mins). Bring in someone to inspire the guests with a short, relevant message. They should preferably provide a Biblical basis for God's saving love and share their story of discovering it.

- **Response** (5 mins). Have an acoustic act sing or play a mellow song. Create a space for any young people who want to respond.

- **Freestyle footballer performs again** (20 mins).

- **End** (10 mins).

Please remember that follow up is especially important. Make sure there is something in place where people can begin a journey of discovery; do not think that just inviting them to a church service or group is enough.

We have found that booking some form of entertainment can be a great way to invite people from the wider community to engage with your church or organisation. Since we are in the business of bringing life to our communities, I would strongly recommend booking someone or something that is as energetic, enthusiastic, and as far different from your normal services or events as possible. For the last Who Loves You? week, we organised a big UV party and booked a live dubstep DJ. One young lady reported it was the best night of her life. We believe that becoming a Christian is to become more alive, so we structure our events to represent that belief. In the past we have also booked freestyle footballers and hip hop artists.

In our experience, the end event works better if you promote it during the week by taking the band/artist (or whatever entertainment form you will be using for your event) with you if you can. Use them to draw attention in whatever context you are promoting and any other forum you can get them into.

NB: Very few people will ever go to an event of a band/ artist or performer that they have never heard of – using the band in this capacity overcomes that obstacle.

Video

A video can be a great way to unpack the question a little more and provoke deeper thought within all the forums you are working in during the week. In our resource pack we have included some examples of the videos we have made in the past, but we suggest you make your own for the week. Your creativity and unique understanding of the people in your area can often be much more effective than what we have made for the areas in which we are working.

We have created intro and outro segments with the BYL branding for you to top and tail a video. These can be found at www.becauseyoureloved.com/how. So all you need to do is script, record, and piece together 1-2 minutes of content that unpack the question. We suggest recording it as a silent movie and using a music track over the top. It is much easier to get good quality pictures than to get good quality sound for vocal recording.

We recommend that the video is no longer than 21/2 minutes long. Any longer than that may cause you to lose people's attention.

Volunteers

Social media is a huge part of contemporary culture. As video making is becoming easier with the use of mobile phones and computers, making videos is now almost second nature for many people.

Sharing stories of how God's love changes lives is a huge part of Who Loves You? Week. In this way, volunteers are asked to make their own 1 minute video of discovering God's love. The videos can then be shared on social media using #becauseyoureloved.

This video should take the following format:

- Volunteer holds up a card with the Who Loves You? logo.

- Then turns the card around, which says, "I heart you."

- Story opens with volunteer saying, "I love you because someone first loved me. Here is my story . . ."

- Volunteer shares their story of discovering God's love for 1 minute.

- Volunteer closes with, "That's my story, and that could be your story, too. I dare you to ask yourself this question. Who Loves You?"

- As they ask the question, volunteer holds up the Who Loves You? logo card again, and the video closes after 10 seconds

Here is an example of Anna Lena's story:

> *"We love because someone first loved us and this is my story. I grew up in a family who went to church and I have been a Christian from a very young age. So I knew of God, but I hadn't really experienced something of Him. But one day when I was eleven, I was in Sunday school and I saw this big picture which was like a canyon and God was on the one side and we were on the other side. Jesus came and with his death on the cross he made a bridge from our side to God so we can come to God. Since I became friends with God I have seen many amazing things and it is always an adventure with Him. That's my story and that could be your story too. I dare you to ask yourself, Who Loves You?"*

Printing

With volunteers signed up and organisation getting under way, it's time to get printing! Free printable resources can be found at www.becauseyoureloved.com. We strongly recommend professional printing to ensure high quality. It may also be advisable to print more than you expect to need. The four things that need to be printed are:

- **Posters**. The idea behind these simple posters is to print them and get as many of them in as many visual places as possible to create a talking point and get the question out in the community.

- **BYL cards**. Make sure your volunteers have BYL cards to use during the week. The BYL cards (business card size and at least five for each volunteer) are designed to be given out along with an act of kindness to spread some love.

- **Who Loves You? thick wristbands**. These are designed to create a talking point/opportunity to share stories and they directly relate to the poster graphic. They are usually available from most good custom wristband suppliers.

- **Tickets**. Usually we print tickets to give out for the invitational. Because tickets give greater credibility than flyers, they tend to generate more excitement for the event. We give them away free in every and any environment we work in: schools, churches, streets, coffee shops, work places, etc. We also give five to each volunteer and encourage them to invite five friends. You can find an example of one of our ticket graphics in the resource pack. (Please note that if you choose to use it, you will need to edit the template to add the dates and venue for your event.)

Guerilla Marketing

Guerilla marketing is a term used for creative, unconventional marketing campaigns, usually run on very low budgets. Where normal marketing campaigns rely on slick communication, glossy images, and very polished execution, guerilla marketing relies on curiosity, innovative creativity, and volume of execution.

Here are some ideas we have used before:

- Poster campaigns

- Street chalk art

- Shop window displays

- Costume promotions

- Art installations

- Mobile billboards

- Outdoor video projection onto architecture

Whenever we chose where to place any of our ideas, we used two very important questions to help us be as strategic as possible. Number one: who is our target audience with whom we want to engage? And number two: where do those people regularly pass or spend time? These questions helped us figure out that the most strategic place we could get the word out was the place that our target audience passed regularly. As a result, as a youth ministry, we often focus our marketing efforts in a busy shopping centre through which young people pass at least twice a day going to and from school.

You can find free electronic copies of all of the cards, posters, and graphics in the WLY? resource pack via www.becauseyoureloved.com/how. We strongly advise using a professional print company to ensure quality.

Bring the Love

Bring the Faith

Bring the Love (BTL) goes beyond a culture of invitation to a proactive practice of bringing. It emboldens people to go the extra mile, to take Jesus to their friends and their friends to Jesus, inspiring a culture of audacious, tenacious, and selfless love.

Have you ever invited someone to church or a church event? It's nerve-wracking, right? It feels like a huge risk. It feels like it could undo all the hard work we've put into blending in. Despite our fears, many of us have done it and experienced the relief and elation of hearing a yes, only to experience the disappointment of a no-show.

I love the story, though, of the friends who brought their mate to Jesus in Mark 2. We don't know how far they carried him or what they knew of Jesus, we just know they were desperate for their friend to meet Jesus. It is a truly beautiful story of sacrifice, healing, and for-giveness. But all that beauty aside, there is something truly profound staring us in the face. The friends didn't simply invite their friend to come see Jesus with them. They physically picked their friend up and brought him to meet Jesus, and when they couldn't find room, they made room. Bring the Love is about going beyond invitation and doing whatever it takes for those we wish to meet Jesus to meet Him. A friend of mine is one of the boldest evangelists I know. A little while ago, he felt God was directing him to go and share God's love with anyone who would listen on a particular street in our town. This street is mainly back-to-back bars and run-down betting shops, and it has somewhat of a reputation for being connected to certain notorious groups of people in the town.

Not long after arriving for the first time, a big guy walked out one of the bars, pointed to my friend's small speaker through which he was playing some music, and told him if he didn't turn it off he was going to smash his head in. Needless to say, his initial response to being asked if he knew God loved him was less than friendly. As he began to get more and more angry, literally shouting in my friend's face with his head pressed against his, God spoke. My friend simply asked, "Do you have a bad back?" Stunned, the angry man calmed and asked how he knew. My friend explained that God had shown him He wanted to heal him, and there in the street as he prayed, the pain and discomfort the man had felt for years faded. At this point the man walked back into the bar, which he turned out to own, and began to tell everyone what just happened. My friend was invited in to pray for whoever wanted it.

Not too long ago, I sat in the same row as this man at church. My friend had been inviting him for weeks to no avail, but that morning he had gone out of his way to pick him and his wife up, and together they experienced something of God's presence afresh that morning.

Each week in one of our gatherings, an entire row is usually taken up by a young lad and his friends. Sounds pretty normal, except usually these aren't necessarily the same friends each week and very often they invite Jesus to be part of their lives; many times it is their first time in a church environment. I am continually inspired by how many of his friends he brings to meet Jesus. Recently I heard the group had grown so large that they now often come together as a bus full and he arranges for all his friends to be picked up if they need a lift. It is fantastic to watch him unlock his world as a Kingdom carrier by bringing his world to an environment where he trusts they will meet Jesus.

Perhaps, though, it raises an awkward question: are our environments places where people can meet Jesus? I'm not sure I have always been able to answer that question honestly with a yes. The heart behind BTL is not simply to boost numbers in our weekly activities or environments, but to facilitate life changing encounters through simply going beyond invitation to bringing.

Bring the Love Week

It is a simple act to facilitate a deep encounter. Bring the Love goes beyond a culture of invitation to a proactive practice of bringing. It emboldens people to both take Jesus to their friends and their friends to Jesus.

BTL centres around the idea that bringing is more powerful than invitation alone. We see this in Mark 2:1-12 when the friends bring their friend to Jesus and are so desperate for him to meet Jesus that when they couldn't find a way through the crowded room, they took him up onto the roof and dug a hole through which they lowered him down. For their friend, invitation just wouldn't have been enough; he needed them to pick him up, carry him, and do whatever it took to make an encounter possible, and for many people in our worlds it is the same.

BTL is probably the most simple, but still creative, programme that runs throughout seven days of a complete week. Volunteers are empowered to bring their friends to social, study, and service-oriented events. Essentially, Bring the Love is the simple act of bringing people to an experience of God's love through three different environments.

Launch Night

Similar to DTL, the BTL Launch Night can be run as part of your regular weekly meeting and is the main opportunity for you to explain the principle and reasoning behind the initiative. The launch will also unpack your chosen events.

Events

To get started, create three events that volunteers can bring people to. As mentioned above, these could be in the context of social, study, and service. Second, you need to promote and gather, equip, empower, and send out your volunteers. While I have included some examples of the three types of events, I would like to encourage you to produce something tailored for your own area.

- **Social**. Socials are great for helping newcomers connect in a fun and easy environment. The relationships formed at socials are a great stepping stone for bringing the person to the next event. This is a great first point of contact!

- **Study**. You may want to call this something like 'Explore' or a name that your church already uses to encourage people to attend who might not be used to the idea of 'study.' It is a place which encourages them to ask a little bit more about who God is. We do this through the Pais Movement's catalytic programme of study called Haverim groups. Haverim simply means "friends who study together." These groups meet weekly to explore and discover God's heart for our lives, our communities, and the wider world context through His Word. They are fun and interactive environments where, through four different fresh approaches to scripture, students learn to dig deeper and explore the Bible for themselves. If you want to find out more about Haverim, then please take a look at www.haverimdevotions.com

- **Service**. This should give people an experience of the Kingdom of God while doing something practical to serve others. It will give them an opportunity to see God work through them by showing His love to others. This could range from street clean ups or reclaiming derelict land to serving in a food bank or homeless shelter.

Before you begin promoting, you need to organise and/or select the three events you will bring people to. Remember, each event should be unique: one social, one study, and one service-oriented. Once these are finalised, you need to start promoting. Starting promotion at least one month in advance is ideal.

VIP Cards

The VIP cards are super simple but one of the most important parts of BTL. The VIP cards are intended to be used to give people the specific details of when and where each of the events take place. They also provide the volunteer's contact information to the person they wish to bring so they can get in touch to liaise lifts or meeting them first.

Pick Up Points

The emphasis is to help people bring their worlds to environments where they can encounter Jesus, so we do recommend creating pick up points either through car-pooling or minibuses where perhaps people can meet their friends and bring them along. These could geographically work in a number of ways, perhaps outside their well-known local landmarks.

NB: Don't worry if for your first project you aren't able to run all of the events, gatherings, or promotions that we have suggested. We have run all of these things in many businesses, schools, and communities and in partner-ships with various agencies and establishments around the world, so we know they work, but some of the success has been because it has been based on years of built-up trust. All of the suggestions serve a purpose but we are also very aware that decisions regarding their go-aheads are often not entirely in our hands. So if for whatever reason it is not possible to run any of the things we have suggested, I would recommend taking the principle and figuring out another way to facilitate that happening. It is not *how* they are delivered that is important; it is *why* they are delivered, which usually fits into two main purposes: to introduce the gospel or to promote a gathering/environment where we can introduce the gospel.

Free electronic templates of the VIP cards and BTL graphics can be found in the BTL resource pack located at www.becauseyoureloved.com/how. We strongly recommend using a professional printing company to ensure quality.

Part 3

What It Takes

Preparation

This part of the book is designed to help you organise and will hopefully be useful for planning a successful project yourself! We would recommend starting to organise a BYL week at least two months before you intend to run it!

One of the best things to do first would be to download the resource pack for the project you wish to run. The resource packs for each of the project weeks are available as free downloads via www.becauseyoureloved.com/how.

Projects

Clarity is our best friend when organising projects. The clearer we are, the better we are able to communicate the purpose, projects, and details to potential participants, partners, and any interested media platform.

Three questions I always ask are:

- **What is my main aim?** What are the intended achievements through the project? Once that is decided, then we build our ideas around it.

- **What will engage the most people?** We live in a culture where people have multiple options; there are probably any number of things they could be doing besides engaging with the project. I usually find stories of success, stories of what could happen, and fun are key ingredients for engaging people.

- **Who are my key leaders?** There are certain people who, if they are engaged first with an idea, they will automatically engage a group of their friends and peers. If possible, take time to pitch the idea to them first and invite them to contribute to helping shape a project. This will give them a sense of ownership that will in turn motivate them to engage other people.

Promo

Promotion of your project is key to each of these weeks. The effectiveness of your promotion will directly affect the success of your weeks!

I know it may sound obvious, but before you can begin promoting, you need to pick and finalise a suitable week to run your project, as well as booking and organising a Launch Night at the start of the week. Once your date and timeframe is finalised, you need to start promoting! Starting promotion at least one month in advance would be ideal. Unfortunately there is no one miracle method for promotion. It takes hard work, but quantity is the key to your material being seen in many forms and in many places.

- Promote the week everywhere possible. Use word of mouth, flyers, PowerPoint, tickets, social media (use #becauseyoureloved), posters, adverts, and whatever else you can think of, wherever you can to get the word out! Don't miss an opportunity to get people involved or supporting!

- Recruit volunteers. The project relies on volunteers getting involved (as many as you can find), so take any opportunity to get them signed up! To do this, we would recommend printing and using a registration list. There are several keys to getting volunteers to sign up:

- Be enthusiastic and positive about your project.

- Be clear about what you're inviting them to be part of.

- There is a fine line between too little and too much repetition; make sure your team are reinforcing your repetition.

- A personal invite can be brilliantly empowering.

- An email invitation can be a great reminder.

- Sometimes people might miss key information weeks, so a good old fashioned mailout can be really effective to catch people up and sometimes even re-engage people.

- Use eye-catching, high-resolution graphics to create a flyer and to use as an invitation.

- Remind from the front in all your environments and in conversation as much as possible.

- NB: In my experience, social media is a great tool for promotion, and #becauseyoureloved has been very successful in spreading the word, but sometimes creating a Facebook event can give us an inflated sense of promotion. 5,000 people may have been invited, but this seldom translates into the real world other than serving as a reminder and a repetition of other forms of invitation which are all super important.

- Once you have volunteers signed up, work out which parts of your community you want to engage.

- Make connections with your community, e.g. schools, universities, or retail districts. Working with an environment like these during the week will give your volunteers a focus point, as well as allowing you to take this opportunity to share your message about God's love in your field of ministry! Book whatever you can and are equipped to do (assemblies, lunch activities, lessons, workshops, or social action like litter picking, painting, cleaning, etc.).

Approach

If you choose to approach a public environment like schools, businesses, universities, retail outlets, or other public environments, it is worth remembering that wherever they are in the world, they exist to enrich their students' lives through education or to make a profit from serving their clients. If you can help them to understand how your project will add value to their students' education or clients' experience, then they will be much more likely to invite you in. In Pais' experience in countries like the USA, where the church and the state are specifically separate, we know this can appear to be more difficult, but we know it is possible as our teams have done it. The key is to work with your volunteers to create opportunities where they can be allowed to invite you in.

Having worked as a Pais missionary in schools and communities all over the UK for ten years and as a student mentor in an inner city high school in Manchester for four years, I noticed there are often two negative misconceptions of churches we have to overcome and they are certainly not isolated to the education sector either.

Firstly, churches can often be considered heavy handed and out of touch. There is a long history, certainly in the UK, of the turn-or-burn evangelists and many public establishments shy away from anything that appears overly heavy-handed as such.

Secondly, non-professionals (i.e. if we are not qualified counsellors, contractors, educators, etc.) are often considered to potentially be overly friendly, chaotic, and unfocused and therefore a relative liability.

So we do several things when approaching schools to try and overcome these misconceptions. The same principles translate across the board as useful in corporate and other public environments.

We approach the top of the food chain first if possible and specifically ask to arrange an in-person meeting. The first step of building trust is building relationship.

- For the introductory meeting, we dress smart; usually that means no jeans and no t-shirts. We dress to the standard the environment expects their staff to dress. It shows respect and professionalism.

- We take examples of our proposals to demonstrate that there is substance to our content. I recommend you research as much as possible before a meeting so you can use your knowledge of their context to explain how your project will enhance, not hinder, their situation.

- We take references which show that we are a credible organisation that provides a service of excellence. If you are just starting out, I would suggest at the very least you can take references from people who have in some way benefited from you before.

- We ensure all of our representatives know exactly what we offer, both so they can communicate clearly and be flexible where possible, but also so they do not agree to anything we cannot deliver with excellence or wisdom.

- When carrying out any of our projects, our teams always wear an easily identifiable uniform and we communicate this clearly during the meeting so that they know.

There are currently Pais teams working throughout the world on six continents and we have found these principles to work in every context our teams have approached. Personally, I find building relationship and trust the most important part of the process, so I rarely mention what we are offering in the first half of a meeting; I don't let my eagerness to get our ministry booked get in the way of building relationship.

When we are working within any context, we highly value four things: excellence, fun, depth, and interaction. So in the planning stages, we are looking to tick those boxes with each piece of ministry. It is also worth noting:

- Participants respond to the tone you set.

- Open-ended questions are one of the best ways to get people to engage.

- We're not there to teach about God; we're there to introduce people to God.

Challenging behaviour or voicing different opinions are not necessarily a sign of failure. (Many times those who've appeared to be the most opposed have been the first to engage more.)

Part 4

Who Can Do It

Resolve

Risk

Because BYL is about sharing God's love through encounters, I am aware that it seems like I'm asking us to take huge risks. And honestly, it raises certain awkward questions.

Questions like, what if the opportunity to pray for someone arises and we pray but nothing happens? Worse still, what if we encourage people to pray and nothing happens? What if we try to engage someone in conversation and they say something mean? What if we meet the minority of miserable people who don't like generosity?

I don't blame anyone for asking questions like that. It is a very realistic possibility. However, each of those possibilities carry the potential for breakthrough in their own way. How we deal with disappointment either propels or repels us to or from breakthrough.

When I have had the opportunity to pray for healing for someone, there have been times I have seen them instantly healed. There have been times when I have seen it happen over a number of hours, days, or even weeks. Still, there have been times when nothing appears to change at all. There have been times I have been accused of using young people as a gimmick. There have been times we have been completely ignored or, worse, sworn at or spat at. I couldn't tell you what was different about each time. I pray my best prayer, I smile my best smile, and I leave it up to God. I have seen people who deny the existence of God get healed and people who seemingly have bucket loads of faith not healed. For none of them can I give you a water-tight explanation of why. However, I do know one thing: things have only changed when we dared to take Jesus at His Word.

For years I wrestled with this issue.

Every summer, my friends and I would head to Christian summer camps where, apart from BMX-ing, skateboarding, and basketball, we would get fired up during the meetings and discover God afresh each year.

At age sixteen, during one such meeting, I felt prompted to pray for my friend's leg. He had been run over a number of years previously and his leg had been so badly damaged surgeons had removed muscles from his back to replace damaged muscles in his ankle. Ever since, he had to wear an uncomfortable splint and walked with a limp. I was fired up and I was convinced this was the night God was going to heal him. So we prayed. We must have prayed for about thirty minutes. Everyone started packing up for the night, and we got more passionate ... but still nothing happened. Nothing had happened by the morning either, nor by the afternoon ... and then something happened. Sadly, it wasn't healing; instead, in a burst of enthusiasm, he kicked a stray football and hit the ground in agony. Somehow the force of kicking the ball broke his weakened ankle and our hope and faith were crushed.

I tried to hide it as best as I could but I was bitterly disappointed. I couldn't understand; I had been certain God was going to heal him, but instead he was worse. I tried to reconcile my disappointment, convincing myself that maybe because we now had doctors, God didn't need to heal anymore. Almost ten years later a friend of mine with some back problems visited a ministry called Healing on the Streets. These people set up in all weathers on high streets all over the world and offer to pray for healing for people and God regularly shows up and heals many who are prayed for. The stories he came back with bugged me because they presented me with a challenge I did not wish to face. They presented me with a different option than disappointment: determination!

Whenever nothing changes, we are faced with a choice: retreat in disappointment or contend and advance with determination.

What would have happened if the disciples had refused to pray for healing or take risks after they had tried healing the young boy we read about in Matthew 17?

> *"When they came to the crowd, a man approached Jesus and knelt before him. 'Lord, have mercy on my son,' he said. 'He has seizures and is suffering greatly. He often falls into the fire or into the water. I brought him to your disciples, but they could not heal him.'" (Matthew 17:14-16)*

Acts 3 could have been a completely different read. Imagine if instead of the incredibly beautiful story of healing and restoration it tells, if it actually read:

> *One day Peter and John were going up to the temple at the time of prayer—at three in the afternoon. Now a man who was lame from birth was being carried to the temple gate called Beautiful, where he was put every day to beg from those going into the temple courts. When he saw Peter and John about to enter, he asked them for money. Peter looked straight at him, as did John. Then Peter looked at John and with a sigh said, "What if nothing happens again?" John went white and just shook his head. The pair of them edged away, smiling their politest smiles, and went about their*

business, trying to forget the desperate look they had seen in the man's eyes.

Not quite so compelling.

Good thing they did not let disappointment hold them back.

The reality is that when we take risks there is no way of avoiding the possibility of disappointment. But how we respond has everything to do with the results we see. Retreat in disappointment or contend and advance in determination? The choice is ours.

Psychological studies show we are raising a risk-averse generation. All too often this has and is infecting the Church.

Recently I took my two oldest boys out to town. We joined with a handful of others to go and drop off snack packs and chocolate around shops and businesses on our local high street. Every month with Allstars (our children's team at Causeway Coast Vineyard) and our Pais Ireland team, we gather a small group who wants to share God's love with our community in one simple way or another. My boys love it! They love being gener-ous and making people smile as they give them a small gift or something. I love it too! I love hanging back and watching them discover they can bring a smile to their world through generosity and love, one simple act at a time. I love watching them have fun while they do it. I love watching them interact with the older young people who are there helping and who set great examples of what it means to love God and love the world around them.

But most of all I love watching something come alive in them as they do it. I have to be honest, my boys are typical young boys. They are not exactly the little angels their disarming smiles would have you believe. They have a habit of speaking their mind and spend most of their lives in a heap on top of each other, wrestling either for fun or a favourite toy. Sometimes I feel more like a referee than a parent, but in amongst all their energy and mess is a hidden treasure, a deposit of the Kingdom, and it comes alive at times like these. One of the most beautiful things about the Kingdom is that it has been entrusted to young and old alike. I find it amazing that in all His glory the Father has trusted His Kingdom to such as these. I barely trust my boys to load the dishwasher!

In Luke 18:15-16 we read:

> "People were also bringing babies to Jesus for him to place his hands on them. When the disciples saw this, they rebuked them. But Jesus called the children to him and said, 'Let the little children come to me, and do not hinder them, for the kingdom of God belongs to such as these.'"

When I take my two boys out and the others with us, it's not some kind of gimmick, nor do I desire for them to stop being kids and immerse themselves in 'church' activity. But it is an opportunity for them to come alive as they engage in generosity, love, and kindness, the culture of Heaven. And so we found ourselves on a cold, wet, windy, Irish afternoon, handing out snack bags and chocolate, spreading some love and hope in our local tattoo parlour, knitting shop, music shop, sports shop, hunting shop, and many other local businesses. We found ourselves engaging in conversation with people we would not usually meet and, as opportunity arose, praying for people about situations that seem utterly hopeless for those without Jesus. That is the beautifully simplistic thing about the Kingdom. It doesn't take a rocket scientist to give it away! Anyone can do it.

Imagine what our communities might look like if we embrace risk and resolve to advance with determination beforehand, to contend for breakthrough come what may, and trust and empower our young people to do the same?

Comfort

Similarly, a lifestyle of sharing God's love may not be pretty and it may not come as neatly packaged as we would like. When we dig into the scriptures we find many paradoxes, but one in particular we seem to polarise on as a wider Church community concerning our identities. We find much in the Bible that suggests that as adopted children of the King of Kings, we are adopted into a royal family, coheirs with Christ as Paul the Apostle puts it. But Paul also sets out a clear mandate for us to serve and live as soldiers of Christ. How can we be both? One suggests luxury, abundance, and prosperity and the other suggests hardship, battle, and struggle.

I think the life of Paul the Apostle, helps give us some indication. The highs and lows of his ministry that followed his conversion and his role in the establishment and growth of the early Church have inspired and encouraged missionaries for thousands of years . . . But they do present somewhat of a problem in the context of popular, contemporary teaching on prosperity and abundance. To clarify, I don't disagree with much prosperity teaching on abundance, but I am fascinated with how we can reconcile prosperity, abundance, and adoption into the Father's royal family with one of the heroes of the Bible's many experiences of imprisonment, hunger, shipwrecks, and beatings.

Interestingly, it often seemed at the very time Paul was most distant from abundance and prosperity is where God provided and fulfilled one of Jesus' promises.

It appears to me that whilst I am sure God loves to bless us with abundance and prosperity as His adopted children . . . He also loves to pursue the lost, the sick, and the broken!

From what I can understand, most often He asks for this to happen through us, His children . . . And that often requires a soldier-like attitude and determination to grit our teeth and push through, whatever it takes, the highs and lows, to bring life to the lost, the sick, and the broken of our worlds. Soldiers by choice give up their peace, safety, normality, comfort, and loved ones, embracing hardship and danger to go into battle. Could it be that God asks us as sons and daughters to do the same at times, giving up our comfort for the sake of welcoming more brothers and sisters into His family? Frequently, the comfort we are asked to give up is not physical, but emotional. Will we choose to lay aside pride and risk looking foolish for the sake of the gospel?

Not long ago, on my way back from a walk along our local beach one evening, I passed a man just relaxing, looking out over the beach and smoking a cigarette. As I passed, I felt the gentle tug on my heart that I have come to recognise as God's prompting. I stopped, self-consciously introduced myself, and began conversation. I hate meeting new people. Everything in me feels uncomfortable and awkward, but long ago I decided His love is more important than my preferences. Our world desperately needs ordinary people in ordinary contexts to move out of our comfort zones to carry the life-changing hope of our Saviour into the storms of life.

Lifeboats

A few years ago I read an article about a luxury cruise liner that hit rocks and sank just off the coast of Tuscany, Italy. In short, a summary of the article was that the captain of the large cruise liner had been arrested for abandoning his post and later released on house arrest after, in January 2012, the ship hit rocks just off the coast of Tuscany. It was carrying more than 4,000 passengers. After hitting the rocks, the captain left the ship and sailed to safety in a lifeboat, while most of his passengers were left onboard the cruise liner as it steadily sank.

Recently we moved house, but we used to live in Portrush, Northern Ireland, where, in the local harbour, the lifeboat that covers the whole of the North Coast is moored. One of my neighbours was part of the crew for the North Coast lifeboats. Every time they are called out to a rescue, they leave at the drop of a hat, all hours of the day, in all weathers, very often risking their own lives.

As analogies, these two present us with a somewhat awkward challenge. My hope is we position our ministries to reflect the selfless attitude of the coast guards and we propel people who have discovered Jesus as the incredible saviour He is out of their metaphorical harbours and into the storms of their worlds to carry a lifeline to all who will engage!

We must refuse to complacently watch our world sink from the safety of our Christian gatherings. Our world needs ordinary people in ordinary environments to carry the lifelines of our extraordinary God, carrying hope, healing, and redemption into the middle of their storms.

In our desire to protect people from the temptations or dangers of the world many times we create safe places for them to come and hang out. We create safe opportunities for them to learn our beliefs. We create bite size devotionals and we create safe Christian communities for them to connect with. But people, especially the growing generation of millennials, crave adventure, passion, participation, authenticity, and experiences. You only have to look at popular fiction or media to understand this.

By the age of thirteen, I had climbed the highest mountains in England, Wales, and Scotland; I had been on more BMX and mountain bike explorations than I could count; I had been to my first rock concert, where the music was so loud the walls shook; I had tried surfing, sea canoeing, kayaking, and much more. Why? Because my dad understood young men love adventure. Admittedly, I managed to break my left elbow in six places, cultivated a deep loathing for holly bushes, and still bear the scars of many other mishaps, but I loved every minute of it. I know my childhood was deeply enriched by the adventures my dad took me on.

Faith adventures provide a wealth of spiritual enrichment, including experiential proof that what's in the Bible is really true and the experiential proof that God is alive and at work in our world today.

Sadly, men and women who have got stuck at the facts and theories fill many seats in our churches. They have knowledge of the stories and teachings of the Bible but have no experiences of their own. No experiences that the God who healed the blind in the Bible still heals today, or the God who fed the 5,000 still provides today, or the God who set people free from demonic captivity still does that today. And history is in danger of repeating itself for future generations. Or should I say, Biblical history is in danger of not repeating itself!

This is increasingly obvious when I am interviewing young adults for placements on our year out programme. Some simply have no stories of their own. Some mistakenly think I am looking for dramatic stories like stories of personal addiction to freedom. That could not be further from the truth. For many, I hope and expect this is not the case. But I do expect stories of God alive and at work. Whatever their background, I do expect to hear stories of God's healing, God's faithfulness, God's provision, God's comfort, God speaking, or God moving in some way or another.

I hope BYL mobilises people young and old to embrace a rescue operation for their worlds. And through this they discover and prove that God is alive and at work, that faith works, and that Christianity is far from a belief system but a captivating, adventurous, exhilarating relationship.

That is, after all, what we believe, right?

Long may we come alive and may our worlds come alive as we engage with the culture of Heaven and see His will done here on earth as it is in Heaven. Long may our hearts resonate with the nearness of the Kingdom, refusing to be held back by risk or polarisation. Long may we pursue the adventure of making His Kingdom our primary concern and mobilising our lives according to His heart for humanity. Long may we facilitate encounters and long may we equip those who come alive through encounters to share their discoveries. Long may God's love transform our world!

Contact

To think through how Because You're Loved can work in your context, check out our Livewire video workshop via becauseyoureloved.com/how. You can also see examples of various Because You're Loved projects in real time through #becauseyoureloved on Twitter and Facebook.

If you are running a Because You're Loved week, we would love for you to get in touch! Ideally, if you can tell us where you are running the week and give us some contact information (name, phone number, and email), it would be helpful. This way, if anyone gets in contact with us about the week or we have any updated information, we can contact you. To do this, please make sure you head over to our website, becauseyoureloved.com.

Besides that, if you have any questions, ideas, or problems regarding the project, please feel free to get in touch. You can send us an email at contact@becauseyoureloved.com

www.becauseyoureloved.com

www.facebook.com/becauseyoureloved

www.twitter.com/bylstories

#becauseyoureloved

About the Author

Mark and Beccy Riley serve as Directors of the Pais Movement in Northern Ireland, living in the beautiful North Coast area. Having been married for over a decade now, they have a young family of three boys, Zach, Levi, and Micah. Together they have over fifteen years of experience working as missionaries and as part of church leadership teams in  Croydon, Manchester, and Northern Ireland. Having used performing arts for a large part of that time, Mark and Beccy are passionate about innovation and creativity.

In 2010, Mark and Beccy began Because You're Loved with Pais Ireland, aiming to provide simple tools for people to share God's love with their worlds. BYL started with just seventy-five volunteers and has now been adopted by the Pais Movement throughout the world. In December 2015, BYL received the award for "Best Youth Work Resource of 2015" from Premier Youth Work at the Christian Youth Work Awards. Over the course of 2015, over 4,000 volunteers were equipped and released to share God's love with their worlds through BYL.

Through their role as Pais Movement Directors, Mark and Beccy now spend most of their time training, equipping, and mobilising individuals to connect and engage in local communities throughout Northern Ireland. Mark is also part of the staff team at Causeway Coast Vineyard Church where he oversees their schools outreach through the work of their two Pais teams.

Mark regularly teaches on themes like everyday mission, adventurous faith, and mission strategies. The last fifteen years on mission has been a roller coaster of an adventure for the Rileys and their stories of risk, breakthrough, healing, and creativity have inspired thousands to take God at His word and take the next steps in their own life adventure.

In his spare time, Mark enjoys drums, surfing, the gym, music, and upcycling.

www.marknathanriley.com

www.twitter.com/rileydrums

Pais Movement

Because You're Loved is the Pais Movement's catalytic program for facilitating mission.

Our Aim

Pais exists to spark a global movement where the primary concern of God's people is His Kingdom and where they are equipped to advance it in their world. We do this through distinctive approaches to mission, discipleship, and study in the areas of youth and schools, churches, and business.

Our Passion

Pais is the New Testament Greek word for "child" or "child servant to the King." Our motto is "missionaries making missionaries." We are passionate about the people of our world and are desperate to see them in the relationship with God that He intended us to have. We come alongside schools, churches, and businesses in their endeavor to empower people to grow in their understanding and experience of God.

Our Vision

Mission lies at the heart of Pais. We seek to help both the apprentices and those they touch develop missionary hearts, missionary skills, and missionary lives. As each missionary makes a missionary, we see our world change.

www.paismovement.com
www.facebook.com/paismovement
www.twitter.com/paismovment

To learn more about the Pais Movement, watch the documentary.

a film about the four stages of vision

'Inspirational & Informative!'
Based on the book "The Line and the Dot" by Paul Clayton Gibbs

TheSpiritofaPioneerFilm.com
Free to view on **vimeo**

Other Books from
Harris House Publishing

By Paul Clayton Gibbs

The Ancient Trilogy

Haverim

How to help anyone study anything. This unique book takes a 2,000 year old method of Bible study and gives it a modern twist.

Talmidim

How to disciple anyone in anything. This book will teach you how to disciple plus give you a template you can use for any situation. Coming 2017.

The Kingdom Trilogy

The Line and the Dot

A book about the four stages all visionaries will go through. If you have a God-given dream or you asking God for a vision, this is the book for you!

The Cloud and the Line

A book about six Kingdom Principles that can transform your relationship with God from a life of rules to one of love.

The Seed and the Cloud

A book about finding direction in your life. Five diagrams are presented that will help you find your next step.

By Katie Hopmann

The King's Invitation

Follow the travels of a boy on his journey to see the King. Along the way, he meets others who have plenty of excuses not to go with him. Instead, they load him down with well-meaning gifts and advice. It's a lot to carry! Will he make it to the Royal City? Or will he give up?

By Karen Sebastian

The Power of Hope for Prodigals

Discover practical steps to establish hope in the midst of dark times. Learn how to see your child through the Father's eyes. Speak words of hope and encouragement. Prepare the way home—it's shorter than you think. Also available in Spanish.

The Power of Hope in Mourning

True grief is often messy, raw, and random. Waves of sadness can wash over you at any time, threatening to drown you in despair. Hope Catalyst Karen Sebastian teaches you to 'ride' those waves, demonstrating how the very pain that threatens to destroy you can push you into the presence of God where hope and healing await.

Available through harrishousepublishing.com and amazon.com.

Harris House
Publishing

FREE CHRISTIAN
GAP YEAR!
INCLUDING FULL TRAINING, ACCOMMODATION AND MEALS

CHOOSE THE COMMUNITY YOU SERVE:

YOUTH
BUSINESSES
CHURCHES
ORGANIZATION

CHOOSE THE NATION YOU SERVE:

EUROPE
NORTH AMERICA
ASIA
AFRICA
SOUTH AMERICA
AUSTRALIA

www.paismovement.com

16899739R00059

Printed in Poland
by Amazon Fulfillment
Poland Sp. z o.o., Wrocław

Show the faith. Share the faith. Bring the faith.

This simple guide equips groups of believers with the tools to become a catalyst of transformation in their community. Because You're Loved is a series of three programmes designed to bring people of all ages to Jesus. It's an adventure that goes beyond simply serving communities to mobilising them to encounter God. Specifically designed as an alternate approach to mission, Because You're Loved can be done anywhere, at any time, with anyone. Participants take part in dares to engage with the community, share stories of God's love, and bring people to Christ-centred events.

#BecauseYoureLoved

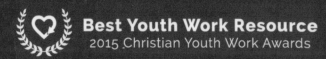

Best Youth Work Resource
2015 Christian Youth Work Awards

" *Because You're Loved is a great platform to work from as it is packed with fun ideas that are just waiting for your creativity to go in the mix.*

Thomas Skov Laugesen
LIFE Church Belfast

Mark and Beccy Riley serve as Directors of the Pais Movement in Northern Ireland and have a young family of three boys. Together they have over fifteen years of experience working as missionaries and as part of church leadership teams.

Harris House Publishing
harrishousepublishing.com

B.Y.L. is a Pais Movement program

$7.5
ISBN 978-0-9862831-8
5075

9 780986 283185